I0605343

CONTENTS

A Much More Exciting Game Comes to Pass

There is nothing in today's NFL that matches the excitement of an exhilarating quarterback-receiver combination. Fans watch in amazement as rocket-armed quarterbacks throw incredible passes from all angles to astonishingly athletic receivers, who make spectacular catches look routine.

A Pass-Catching Phenom

But it was not always so. Ninety years ago, the National Football League (NFL) was a plodding, run-oriented snoozefest. Then, along came star end Don Hutson. The pass-catching phenom revolutionized the game, teaming with star passers Arnie Herber and Cecil Isbell to lead the Green Bay Packers to three NFL championships in a career that lasted from 1935 to 1945. Hutson's statistical dominance of his era was so profound he has been called the Babe Ruth of football—a reference to one of baseball's most iconic players.

Hutson had blazing speed, great hands, and was a pass-pattern pioneer. He made sharp cuts and deceptive moves to get open, innovations that would eventually catch on across pro football. "Hutson is the only man who can feint in three directions at once,"[1] former Philadelphia Eagles coach Earle "Greasy" Neale once said.

Even George Halas, whose Chicago Bears team often battled for the top spot in matchups with the Packers, said of Hutson, "I just concede him two touchdowns a game, and I hope we can score more."[2] But Hutson, with his passing cohorts, accomplished far more than bringing titles to the small Wisconsin city that would become football famous. He changed the understanding of offensive football. No longer were teams limited to grinding, brutal ground movements. They could now see the potential for fast and fascinating air travel. Clearly, this was no passing fancy. Gifted quarterbacks and receivers have been teaming up ever since, thrilling fans with phenomenal feats unimaginable to football's founding fathers.

> **"I just concede him two touchdowns a game, and I hope we can score more."[2]**
>
> —George Halas, Chicago Bears founder and former head coach

Passing the Torch

Talented quarterbacks such as Chicago's Sid Luckman and Washington's Sammy Baugh advanced the NFL passing game during the 1940s. The Cleveland Browns, led by star quarterback Otto Graham and coached by the innovative Paul Brown, took it to new heights. Graham, throwing to outstanding receivers Dante Lavelli and Mac Speedie, reached the championship game in all ten seasons of his pro football career. The Browns showed the football world how effective passing could be, winning all four titles in the All-America Football Conference (1946 to 1949) and then stunning the NFL with three titles during the team's first six seasons in the league (1950 to 1955).

Johnny Unitas and Raymond Berry formed a formidable duo that led the Baltimore Colts to NFL titles in 1958 and 1959. The pair's performance in the 1958 title game, the first NFL playoff game to be decided in sudden-death overtime, launched football on its way to becoming America's favorite sport. The nationally televised game showed Unitas driving the visiting Colts to a tying field goal in the final seconds of regulation play, then orchestrating the winning touchdown drive in overtime for a 23–17 win over the New York Giants. Unitas completed twenty-six of forty passes for 349 yards—huge numbers for the time. Even more astonishing, Berry caught twelve passes for 178 yards and one touchdown, a 15-yarder from Unitas. Berry's twelve receptions set an NFL

Los Angeles Chargers quarterback Justin Herbert (10) passes the ball against the Kansas City Chiefs during a game at SoFi Stadium, August 17, 2024. There are few things in today's NFL that match the excitement of an exhilarating quarterback-receiver combination.

Championship Game/Super Bowl record that was not topped for fifty-five years. "The game captured the collective attention of the nation and as a result, pro football exploded across the country in the following years,"[3] according to the Pro Football Hall of Fame.

The upstart American Football League (AFL), which began play in 1960, tried to win over fans with a more aggressive passing game than was common in the established NFL. The Houston Oilers' George Blanda threw thirty-six touchdown passes in 1961, more than any NFL passer had ever tossed in a season to that point. The New York Jets' Joe Namath became the first quarterback to throw for 4,000 yards in a season in 1967, with his favorite target, Don Maynard, topping pro football with 1,434 receiving yards. The excitement generated by the deep passing games of AFL quarterbacks such as Namath and the Oakland Raiders' Daryle "the Mad Bomber" Lamonica helped lead to the AFL-NFL merger, which took effect before the 1970 season.

A Dangerous Offensive Weapon

Pro football benefited from several passing game gurus, starting with Brown and moving to Sid Gillman in the 1960s, Don Coryell in the 1970s and early 1980s, and Bill Walsh in the 1980s. These coaches all brought strategic changes to the passing game, making it more sophisticated and difficult to defend. Outstanding quarterback-receiver combinations continued to make passing the most dangerous offensive weapon. As Gillman said, "The big play comes with the pass. God bless those runners because they get you the first down, give you ball control and keep your defense off the field. But if you want to ring the cash register, you have to pass."[4]

CHAPTER ONE

Men of Steel: Terry Bradshaw and Lynn Swann

The Pittsburgh Steelers were leading the Dallas Cowboys 15–10 with less than 4 minutes remaining in the fourth quarter of Super Bowl X on January 18, 1976, when Steelers quarterback Terry Bradshaw dropped back to pass. Avoiding hard-charging linebacker D.D. Lewis, Bradshaw unleashed a 60-yard missile down the field into the waiting arms of wide receiver Lynn Swann. The second-year receiver caught the ball inside the 10-yard line and dashed into the end zone for a touchdown, giving the Steelers a 21–17 victory.

But while Swann celebrated, Bradshaw was flat on his back. After throwing the touchdown, the quarterback had taken a punishing hit from defensive lineman Larry Cole. But while Bradshaw did not see the result of his historic throw, the perfect play illustrated how a talented quarterback-receiver combination can succeed in the NFL. As Bradshaw later put it, "I was just going to throw it as far as I could, and Lynn Swann was going to catch up to it."[5]

The touchdown reception capped Swann's four-catch, 161-yard performance in the game, which earned him Super Bowl Most Valuable Player (MVP) honors. Today, Swann's performance remains among the best ever by a wide receiver in a Super Bowl.

Showing Their Championship Mettle

As stellar as the Bradshaw–Swann combination was in Super Bowl X, the team had an entire roster of star players. Offensively, the Steelers' attack was powered by running backs Rocky Bleier and Franco Harris. Wide receiver John Stallworth, like Swann, posed a wide-receiving deep threat. Meanwhile, on defense, the Steelers fielded some of the hardest-hitting players in the NFL, including left tackle "Mean" Joe Greene, linebackers Jack Ham and Jack Lambert, and cornerback Mel Blount. Their fearsome reputation earned them a nickname: the Steel Curtain. Steelers head coach, Chuck Noll, cultivated an atmosphere of team toughness, unity, and resilience.

At the end of Super Bowl X, Bradshaw unleashed a 60-yard missile into the waiting arms of wide receiver Lynn Swann, who ran for a touchdown, giving the Steelers a 21–17 victory.

Yet the aerial exploits of Bradshaw and Swann were what made the television highlight reels during the mid-1970s. Together, they paired up for some of the biggest plays of the 1970s as the Steelers won an unmatched four Super Bowls in six seasons. Although defenses tried to prevent the Steelers' big-play combo from dominating games, Bradshaw and Swann were still able to make the biggest plays in the biggest games no matter how tight the coverage. Swann's incredible jumping ability and great hands enabled him to make spectacular catches over frustrated defensive backs. Bradshaw's phenomenal arm strength allowed him to throw perfect deep balls and to zip passes into tight spaces. The two stars repeated their Super Bowl magic three years later during Super Bowl XIII in January 1979. With the Steelers leading the Cowboys 28–17 in the fourth quarter, Bradshaw fired a pass into the end zone. Swann leaped and made a spectacular catch for the title-clinching 18-yard touchdown. Bradshaw was Super Bowl MVP after throwing for 318 yards and four touchdowns. Swann led all receivers with seven catches for 124 yards in a 35–31 victory.

In Super Bowl XIV the following year, Bradshaw threw for 309 yards and two touchdowns. Swann caught a game-high five passes for 79 yards, including a 47-yard touchdown reception in which he made a leaping catch in between two Los Angeles Rams defenders and carried the ball into the end zone.

Challenges to Champions

Before Bradshaw and Swann became the NFL's most feared big-game passing combination, they both had to grow as players. Bradshaw had been the top overall pick in the 1970 NFL draft. But he was playing for a team that had never won a playoff game, and his inconsistent early performances did not help change the team's fortunes. In 1974, Bradshaw lost his starting job to Joe Gilliam, a major embarrassment for a former number-one pick.

The Danger Zone

The middle of the field was a danger zone for NFL receivers during the 1970s. Tough defensive backs hoped to intimidate or knock out receivers who dared to venture into their territory. But Pittsburgh Steelers star receiver Lynn Swann, blessed with a rocket-armed quarterback in Terry Bradshaw, was not deterred. "I run inside nearly every time," Swann said in January 1979. "Sure, that's where you get hit the hardest. But when you can hang on during the hit, you've gained a lot more than yardage. You've played into the secondary's strength and won, and you leave them with a sinking feeling, you leave them scratching their heads."

Frustrated opponents took extreme measures to try to stop Pittsburgh's top passing combination. Dave Logan, a Cleveland Browns receiver from 1976 to 1983, recalled his team's defensive approach. "There were two guys with the Steelers that guys would openly talk about," Logan said. "If you ever get a shot at Bradshaw, and if you ever get a shot at Swann coming across the middle, we're gonna knock the taste out of his mouth." But, despite the best efforts of the defense, it was usually Bradshaw and Swann who tasted victory.

Quoted in *Sports Illustrated* staff, "Hello, Remember Me? Cowboys Charlie Waters and Cliff Harris Can't Quite Forget Steeler Lynn Swann, Not After What He Did to Them in Super Bowl X," *Sports Illustrated* Vault, January 1979. https://vault.si.com.

Quoted in Matthew Marczi, "Former Browns WR Says Defense Targeted Steelers' Terry Bradshaw, Lynn Swann: 'We're Gonna Knock the Taste Out of His Mouth,'" Steelers Depot, July 3, 2024. https://steelersdepot.com.

Swann, meanwhile, enjoyed a brilliant college career that included a starring role on an undefeated national championship team at the University of Southern California. Swann was drafted by the Steelers during the first round in 1974, but he received little playing time during his first season. The five-foot-eleven, 180-pound rookie worked hard on his game, however, and waited for his chance to play. Swann's bond with Bradshaw began to strengthen in late 1974, and their ascent coincided with the Steelers' rise to the top of the NFL.

The Steelers finished the 1974 regular season with a 10–3–1 record. As the playoffs began, Bradshaw was back as the starter after quarterbacks Gilliam and Terry Hanratty struggled. It quickly became apparent that the resurrected quarterback and the fast-learning rookie wide receiver were ready for the post-season pressure. After trouncing the Buffalo Bills 32–14 in the divisional round of the playoffs, the Steelers headed to Oakland for the American Football Conference (AFC) title game. With the score tied 10–10 in the fourth quarter, Bradshaw connected with Swann on a 6-yard touchdown pass to put the Steelers ahead in a 24–13 victory. The upset catapulted the Steelers to their first Super Bowl, where they scored a 16–6 win over the Minnesota Vikings.

Developing Unsurpassed Connectivity

The Steelers rolled to a 12–2 regular-season record in 1975, beat the Colts 28–10 during the divisional round, and then met the Raiders in an AFC title game rematch. Swann suffered a concussion after a vicious hit during the Steelers' 16–10 win. It seemed unlikely that he would play in the Super Bowl. Yet, after two weeks of rest, Swann proved his resolve by taking the field on January 18, 1976, for Super Bowl X. "I looked at the films of me being carried off and I was limper than a piece of spaghetti," Swann said. "I made a vow then I'd play. Somehow, someway."[6] Bradshaw showed that his confidence in his star receiver never wavered, going to him for some of the biggest plays of the game.

After a 10–4 regular season in 1976, Bradshaw and Swann continued their postseason success in a divisional playoff game against the Baltimore Colts. Bradshaw tossed three touchdown passes in a 40–14 win. Swann caught two of the scoring passes and finished with a team high of five receptions for 77 yards. The Steelers, however, lost to the Raiders in the AFC Championship Game the next week and were defeated in the divisional round by the Denver Broncos the following season.

But the Steelers bounced back with a 14–2 regular season in 1978, and Bradshaw and Swann were on top of their game. The quarterback fired touchdown passes to his top target in two playoff routs as the Steelers barreled into Super Bowl XIII against the Dallas Cowboys. Cowboys safety Charlie Waters hoped the use of extra pass rushers would put pressure on Bradshaw but knew that approach came with great risk against the six-foot-three, 215-pound quarterback. "When you blitz, it's critical that you get to the quarterback quickly," Waters said. "If you leave Swann one-on-one, and Bradshaw sees it, then you might as well forget it. And Terry, being the stud that he is, can hang in there like a big oak tree. Other quarterbacks start falling down when you come near 'em, but Terry never gets off balance."[7]

> **"When you blitz, it's critical that you get to the quarterback quickly. If you leave Swann one-on-one, and Bradshaw sees it, then you might as well forget it."[7]**
>
> —Charlie Waters, former Cowboys safety

The success that Bradshaw and Swann enjoyed together was a result of more than their remarkable physical abilities. Swann talked about the exceptional mental connection he and Bradshaw developed. "There are some balls that Terry throws and I catch that go beyond the timing or even beyond the play itself. It's as though the ball has his force and my force around it.

Standing the Test of Time

The names Terry Bradshaw and Lynn Swann do not appear near the top of modern regular-season passing or pass receiving categories. But that does not diminish the greatness of the former Pittsburgh Steelers quarterback and receiver who combined for some of the most memorable plays of the 1970s.

The Steelers offense, like many others of the era, often depended on the running game. Plus, the Steelers defense, known as the Steel Curtain, was so dominant that there was often no need for the offense to rely on the passing game. Still, when the Steelers needed the biggest plays in the biggest games, it was Bradshaw and Swann who repeatedly came through.

By the time the Steelers won their fourth Super Bowl title in January 1980, Bradshaw and Swann had established themselves as the sport's superstars. Amazingly, their feats have stood the test of time despite the NFL's metamorphosis to a passing-dominated game. Half a century after the Steelers' dynasty began, Bradshaw and Swann remain NFL legends, whose improbable plays and Super Bowl wins are remembered more than individual statistics. That might be the dynamic duo's most impressive accomplishment.

I'll turn when I'm not supposed to turn, or turn early or turn late, and there's the ball. Terry has put my scent on it, and nobody else can possibly catch that ball but me."[8]

> **"There are some balls that Terry throws and I catch that go beyond the timing or even beyond the play itself. It's as though the ball has his force and my force around it."[8]**
>
> —Lynn Swann, former Steelers receiver

Bradshaw, too, noticed something special about the 1978 season. "Last year I throw a pass to Swann, it's a good pass, a good catch, and somebody is right there to tackle him. This year I throw the same pass, and he zigs around four guys and goes into the end zone. Call it luck or magic or whatever. I like it."[9]

Stealing Steelers Fans' Hearts

The Steelers stars continued their playoff dominance the next season, leading to yet another trip to the Super Bowl. In Super Bowl XIV in January 1980, the Steelers concluded their remarkable run with a 31–19 win over the Rams.

The season that followed, in the fall of 1980, marked a turning point though. The defense, once so fearsome, gave up more yards than in many years. And turnovers plagued the team. For the first time since 1971, the Steelers did not reach the playoffs. The team finished the season with a 9–7 record. The next year, 1981, was even worse, with the pride of Steel City ending with an 8–8 record and failing to gain a playoff berth for the second year in a row.

> **"Last year I throw a pass to Swann, it's a good pass, a good catch, and somebody is right there to tackle him. This year I throw the same pass, and he zigs around four guys and goes into the end zone. Call it luck or magic or whatever. I like it."[9]**
>
> —Terry Bradshaw, former Steelers quarterback

The 1982 season saw improvement, with the Steelers reaching the first round of the playoffs, but they lost a tight game to the San Diego Chargers, 31–28. The narrow defeat seemed to mark the end of an era, as the team's glory days seemed to be a thing of the past. Days after the loss, Lynn Swann announced his retire-

Swann (88) and Bradshaw (12) prepare for another play during Super Bowl XIV. The two men provided numerous thrills for fans as the Pittsburgh Steelers became the team of the 1970s.

ment. At the age of thirty, Swann was a four-time Super Bowl champion, Super Bowl X's MVP, and a three-time Pro Bowl selection. Bradshaw remained with the team through 1983, but he suffered an elbow injury and officially retired at the end of the season.

The two men had provided numerous thrills for fans as the Pittsburgh Steelers became the team of the 1970s. Their unprecedented streak of game-turning plays in the most crucial moments was stunning in a time when many teams still relied primarily on the running game. Their clutch performances in exciting Super Bowls helped cement football as America's favorite sport.

CHAPTER TWO

49ers Strike Gold: Joe Montana and Jerry Rice

The San Francisco 49ers trailed the Cincinnati Bengals 16–13 with less than 4 minutes remaining in Super Bowl XXIII. The 49ers were on their own 8-yard line. Some Bengals players celebrated what they thought would be the franchise's first Super Bowl title—but not Bengals receiver Cris Collinsworth. "Are you guys nuts?" Collinsworth recalled saying. "I knew there was too much time left on the clock for [49ers quarterback] Joe Montana."[10] Collinsworth, who went on to a distinguished broadcasting career, could have added "and Jerry Rice"—the famed 49ers wide receiver—to the quote.

Collinsworth's worst fears were realized as Montana calmly drove his team 92 yards to the winning touchdown in a 20–16 win in January 1989. Montana completed eight of nine passes on the pressure-packed drive—three of them to Rice for 51 yards. The winning touchdown came on a 10-yard pass to John Taylor with 34 seconds left, but as usual during San Francisco's 1980s dynasty, it was Montana and Rice taking top billing. Montana completed twenty-three of thirty-six passes for 357 yards and two touchdowns, while Rice finished with eleven receptions for a Super Bowl record of 215 yards and a touchdown. Time after time, when Montana needed a key completion, he went to his favorite target. Rice came through again and again on his way to being named Super Bowl MVP. Montana and Rice won another Super Bowl the following year, when San Francisco crushed Denver 55–10. In that game, Montana completed twenty-two of twenty-nine passes for 297 yards and five touchdowns. Rice caught seven passes for 148 yards. Three of his catches were for touchdowns—a Super Bowl record.

Stars Align to Achieve Greatness

Montana and Rice can stake a strong claim to being the greatest quarterback-receiver tandem in NFL history. Rice, still the NFL's all-time leader in receptions (1,549), receiving yards (22,895) and touchdown receptions (197), is generally considered the best receiver of all time. Montana is consistently ranked among the top three quarterbacks ever.

Together from 1985 to 1990, Rice's precise route running, excellent hands, and ability to run after the catch combined with Montana's uncanny accuracy to make them as close to unstoppable as the league has ever seen. They were the perfect fit for the so-called West Coast offense masterminded by 49ers coach Bill Walsh. Walsh had developed the philosophy when he was an assistant coach in Cincinnati. The innovative scheme relied on quick, shorter passes instead of the running game and deep throws that had dominated the NFL for decades.

> **"Joe Montana and I, we had such chemistry. If Joe was a female, we would have dated because the chemistry was just that [good]."[11]**
>
> —Jerry Rice, former 49ers receiver

Yet Walsh's West Coast offense might not have been as successful if not for the unique blend of players on the squad and the relationships they built with one another. How they interacted on the field and jelled as a team, week in and week out, was as important as the *x*'s and *o*'s used to diagram plays. For his part, Jerry Rice understood the connection he had with his quarterback. "Joe Montana and I, we had such chemistry," Rice recalled. "If Joe was a female, we would have dated because the chemistry was just that [good]. I knew Montana wouldn't hold on to the ball that long. If I ran my routes, I knew the ball was halfway in the air."[11]

Montana and Rice were a team within a team, dominating defenses, running up scores, and leading their team to multiple championships. Montana's ability to remain calm, even under intense pressure from opponents, gave him time to read defenses, find his receivers, and complete passes. The six-foot-two, 200-pound quarterback went 4–0 in Super Bowls, being named MVP in three of those games. Rice, also listed as six foot two and 200 pounds, is the career leader in Super Bowl receptions (33), receiving yards (589), and touchdown catches (8).

Superstar, Newbie Forge Connection

When the 49ers picked Rice in the 1985 draft, Montana was already a two-time Super Bowl champion. But the quarterback's greatest moments were yet to come, largely because of his talented young receiver. The Montana–Rice combination enjoyed a solid first season together, though the receiver later recalled a bumpy beginning. "When I first came in, I said, 'Everything Montana throws me I'm gonna catch it. I got to win his confidence over.' I was catching everything at practice but then during ball games and during preseason, I was dropping everything," Rice said. "I remember getting booed."[12]

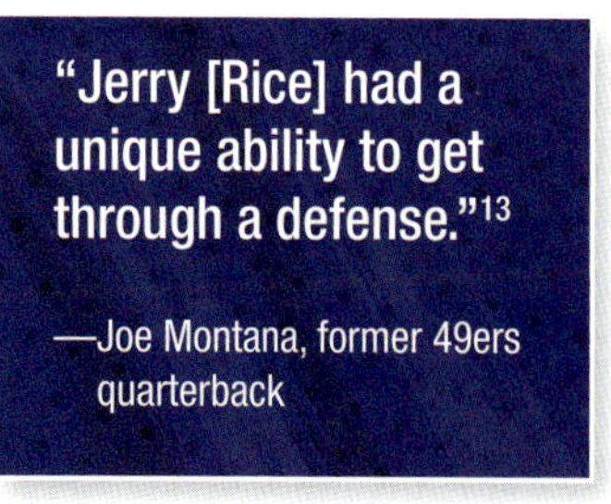
"Jerry [Rice] had a unique ability to get through a defense."[13]

—Joe Montana, former 49ers quarterback

Their teamwork blossomed during their second season together and exploded during year three. During the strike-shortened 1987 regular season, Rice caught an astonishing twenty-two touchdown passes. That total set a single-season record that stood until Randy Moss caught twenty-three scoring passes while playing sixteen games in 2007 with the New England Patriots. Montana led the NFL in 1987 with thirty-one touchdown passes, with most of that success a result of his connection with his star receiver. "Jerry had a unique ability to get through a defense. I don't know what it was," Montana said. "I can't even put a finger on it. He beats more people to the post and across the field than I've ever seen."[13]

Quarterback Joe Montana throws a pass in Super Bowl XXIII. With the 49ers losing 16–13 with four minutes remaining in the game, Montana engineered a 92-yard drive for a game winning touchdown.

Setting the Gold Standard

Despite the stellar performances of Montana and Rice during the 1987 regular season, the top-seeded 49ers were upset by the Minnesota Vikings in the divisional playoffs that year, 36–24. But the following year the duo dominated the 1988 postseason, starting with a 34–9 victory against the Vikings in the first round of the playoffs. Rice caught three touchdown passes from Montana in the first half.

The 49ers' reward was a January 8, 1989, trip to Chicago to face the Bears in the National Football Conference (NFC) Championship Game at Soldier Field. Many thought the frigid Windy City weather would favor the home team. However, it quickly became apparent that neither the Bears' tough defense nor the cold could slow down the Montana–Rice combination. With a 61-yard

Foreshadowing the Future

To hear Joe Montana tell it, Jerry Rice's earliest preseason practices with the 49ers hardly indicated a star in the making. During the summer of 1985, the rookie wide receiver seemed to be trying too hard, resulting in drops, flubbed timing, and balls hitting him in the face. That year the 49ers were the defending Super Bowl champions, but they struggled through their first seven games, losing four of them. Then, in their eighth, against the Rams in Los Angeles, the 49ers found themselves on their own 4-yard line. Montana tossed a slant pass to receiver John Taylor, who ran 96 yards. Jerry Rice, near the end zone, threw a block against the Rams defender and secured Taylor's touchdown. Moments later, he did it again. Such selfless play endeared Rice to Montana, but fans had yet to see his true potential.

A second game against the Rams on December 9, 1985, changed that. Under the lights of Candlestick Park, Montana completed twenty-six of thirty-six passes for 328 yards and three touchdowns. Rice caught ten passes for 241 yards, including a 66-yard touchdown catch. The Rams won the game 27–20, but Montana and Rice had finally given fans a glimpse of the pairing that would dominate the NFL for years to come.

touchdown in the first quarter and a 27-yard score in the second, the pair appeared unstoppable, leading the 49ers to a blowout 28–3 victory. Montana finished seventeen of twenty-seven passes for 288 yards and three touchdowns. Rice caught five passes for a game-high 133 yards.

Two weeks later, the newly crowned NFC champions met their AFC counterparts, the Cincinnati Bengals, in Miami for Super Bowl XXIII. By halftime, each team had kicked field goals. In the third quarter, the Bengals attacked. On their first drive, Bengals quarterback Boomer Esiason completed a handful of passes to his receivers, but the 49ers defense held them to another field goal. A Bengals kickoff return touchdown with less than a minute left in the third quarter widened their lead.

Then, Montana led the 49ers on a four-play, 85-yard drive. The first play of the drive was a short pass to Rice, who broke tackles for a 31-yard gain. A 14-yard touchdown pass to Rice tied the game 13–13 in the fourth quarter. The 49ers took the lead after a 27-yard completion to Rice took them to the Bengals' 18-yard line and was followed by a 10-yard touchdown pass to receiver John Taylor. The superstar Rice was named MVP and finished the game with 215 receiving yards, including a touchdown. Montana racked up 357 passing yards and threw for two touchdowns.

Nobody Does It Better

As the 1989 season began, the NFL's most feared passing combination was peaking. Montana was named the league's MVP for the first time, while Rice led the NFL with seventeen touchdown catches and 1,483 receiving yards. The 49ers went 14–2 during the regular season and again faced the Vikings in the divisional playoffs. In the first quarter, Montana and Rice teamed up

Jerry Rice makes an impossible catch during Super Bowl XXIII. As of 2025, Rice remains the NFL leader in Super Bowl receptions, receiving yards, and touchdown catches.

In a League of Their Own

Joe Montana and Jerry Rice were on top of their game on October 14, 1990, in Atlanta. The incomparable duo put up staggering numbers in an era when passing numbers paled in comparison to today.

Rice caught five touchdown passes from his MVP quarterback in a 45–35 win over the Falcons. The receiver finished with thirteen catches for 225 yards. "Rice is the total package," Falcons cornerback Charles Dimry said. "He has pull-away speed. It's difficult when you're playing one of the best."

Montana set single-game records for the 49ers with 476 passing yards and six touchdown throws. He completed thirty-two of forty-nine passes. "I don't know if a quarterback can play any better," Falcons coach Jerry Glanville said. "He gave us a lesson. My hat's off to the guy. I can't wait until he retires."

Quoted in Joe Hession, "Montana to Rice Times Five," 49ers Museum, November 22, 2021. www.49ers.com.

for a 72-yard touchdown pass to put the 49ers up 7–3. The duo connected again for a 13-yard score to put them ahead 27–3 at halftime. Montana completed seventeen of twenty-four passes for 241 yards and four touchdowns in the 41–13 rout. Rice, as usual, led the 49ers receivers with six catches for 114 yards. A week later, the 49ers crushed the Los Angeles Rams 30–3 in the NFC title game, with Montana completing twenty-six of thirty passes for 262 yards and two touchdowns. Rice contributed six catches for a game-high 55 yards.

Montana and Rice capped their season with stellar performances in Super Bowl XXIV against the Denver Broncos on January 28, 1990. Early in the first quarter, a 20-yard touchdown pass to Rice put San Francisco up 7–0. A 38-yard connection made it 27–3 at halftime, and a 28-yard third-quarter score stretched the advantage to 34–3. The 1990 regular season was similarly spectacular for Montana and Rice. The 49ers again went 14–2, Montana repeated as MVP, and Rice led the NFL with one hundred catches, 1,502 yards receiving, and thirteen touchdown catches. The tandem seemed unstoppable.

Superstars Go Their Separate Ways

Yet while the 1990 regular season had been marked by San Francisco's dominance, the postseason presented unfamiliar challenges. In the divisional playoffs in January 1991, San Francisco met Washington, whose early touchdown and field goal had San Francisco playing from behind, 10–7. Then, in the second quarter, two quick touchdowns from Montana, including a 10-yard scoring pass to Rice, put San Francisco ahead. The team won the game 28–10. But a week later, San Francisco's bid to become the first team to win three consecutive Super Bowls ended in a 15–13 upset loss to the New York Giants in the NFC Championship Game. It also ended an era of unparalleled game play between San Francisco's quarterback and receiver. The next season, Montana played in only one game because of an elbow injury. He played only one game in 1992, was traded to the Kansas City Chiefs, and retired after the 1994 season.

Montana and Rice support each other during a game in 1986. Since retirement, Rice has made it clear that the connection he shared with Montana could not be beat.

Rice, though, remained a 49er. With Montana injured during the 1991 season, his backup, Steve Young, became the team's starting quarterback. Before long, Young and Rice found an on-the-field rhythm that continued the high-scoring performance of one of the league's best teams through the 1998 season.

Jerry Rice remained with San Francisco through the 2000 season, but in June 2001 he was released, making him a free agent. Though slowed by a persistent knee injury, the superstar receiver believed that once healthy he could still help an NFL team win games. The Oakland Raiders agreed and signed Rice a day after San Francisco let him go. During the 2001 and 2002 seasons, Rice proved his critics wrong by catching passes from Oakland's quarterback, Rich Gannon, and racking up 1,000 receiving yards. He spent two final seasons with the Seattle Seahawks before retiring in 2006.

"Joe [Montana] was that competitor that came to play every ball game. And he was going to leave everything out there on the football field."[14]

—Jerry Rice, former 49ers receiver

After leaving the game, whenever Rice was asked about the best quarterback he ever played with, he made it clear that the connection he shared with Joe Montana could not be beat. As Rice recalled years after he and Montana retired, "Joe was that competitor that came to play every ball game. And he was going to leave everything out there on the football field. Great leader. Great friend. Overall, I think he's the greatest football player ever."[14]

CHAPTER THREE

Return to Glory: Troy Aikman and Michael Irvin

From 1966 to 1985, the Dallas Cowboys had been one of pro football's best and most popular teams. But, oh, how the mighty had fallen. During the 1986 and 1987 seasons, the Cowboys struggled with player injuries and weak defenses. After two consecutive losing seasons, in 1988 the Cowboys drafted wide receiver Michael Irvin, hoping that he would bring speed and playmaking ability to the team. Despite Irvin's obvious talents, the Cowboys went 3–13 that year. Desperate to turn things around, the Cowboys went on the hunt for more new talent, someone who could lead the team. In 1989 the team drafted quarterback Troy Aikman, a skilled passer who had been named the country's top college player at his position while at the University of California, Los Angeles. But the much hoped for turnaround did not happen. The slide worsened, with the Cowboys finishing the season with a 1–15 record. The next few seasons were hardly better.

But by January 1993, the Cowboys had returned to the top of the NFL mountain with a lopsided 52–17 win over the Buffalo Bills in Super Bowl XXVII. Aikman was named MVP after completing twenty-two of thirty passes for 273 yards and four touchdowns. Irvin caught two of those touchdown passes and finished with a team-high 114 receiving yards. Aikman and Irvin had plenty of help in the team's meteoric rise from the outhouse to the penthouse.

Coach Jimmy Johnson, who arrived in Dallas in 1989, built a team with a strong offensive line and defense. And when the Cowboys drafted running back Emmitt Smith (who later became the NFL's all-time rushing leader) in 1990, the transformation was complete.

A Strong Bond

By the 1990s the Cowboys were once again winning Super Bowls. While Smith consistently churned out yardage on the ground, Aikman and Irvin combined for big plays in the passing game. Aikman provided great arm strength and accuracy. Irvin supplied detailed route running, superior strength, excellent hands, and unsurpassed competitiveness. They were both outstanding leaders who built a strong bond on and off the field. "There's nothing like standing in that huddle, looking up and [Aikman] saying, 'I'm coming to you,'"[15] Irvin said.

Aikman went to Irvin early and often in the NFC Championship Game in January 1996. Irvin caught two first-quarter touchdown passes and led Dallas with seven receptions for 100 yards during the team's 38–27 win over the visiting Green Bay Packers. Irvin's performance in the win over Green Bay caught no one by surprise. The six-foot-two, 207-pound receiver had his best season in 1995, with 1,603 receiving yards and ten touchdowns.

> **"There's nothing like standing in that huddle, looking up and [Aikman] saying, 'I'm coming to you.'"[15]**
>
> —Michael Irvin, former Cowboys receiver

But what made the dynamic between Aikman and Irvin so special goes way beyond stats. They were both at their best during the biggest moments, regularly combining for decisive plays when the Cowboys needed it most. The six-foot-four, 219-pound Aikman could confidently throw to Irvin in tight coverage because the receiver would always fight for the ball and often come up with big plays. "We've played together so long, it doesn't just happen," Aikman said in a

1997 interview. "Everyone knows we're going to Michael. They move people around to stop him. But he's special."[16] Irvin earned the nickname "the Playmaker" for his great success in exactly these types of pressure situations.

> "Everyone knows we're going to Michael. They move people around to stop him. But he's special."[16]
>
> —Troy Aikman, former Cowboys quarterback

The Players Grow

The growth of the on-field relationship between Aikman and Irvin mirrored that of the Cowboys' ascent. In their first year together, Aikman's rookie season of 1989, they flashed their potential in

Troy Aikman throws a pass during Super Bowl XXVII. The Cowboys went on to win 52–17 and Aikman was named MVP.

A Running Back's Perspective

While Cowboys quarterback Troy Aikman and receiver Michael Irvin combined to put up huge numbers and collaborate on some of the biggest plays of the 1990s, the Cowboys of that era were primarily known as a running team. Their ace in the hole was power back Emmitt Smith, a tough, scrappy, and consistent player. Over fifteen NFL seasons, Smith made the Pro Bowl eight times and was named the Super Bowl MVP in 1994. He remains the NFL's leading rusher with 18,355 yards on the ground and 164 touchdowns. Smith, who was inducted into the Pro Football Hall of Fame in 2010, witnessed the dynamism of Aikman and Irvin early on. In Irvin, Smith later said, the Cowboys not only had a gifted receiver but also a player who became crucial to their success. "Michael Irvin was the most competitive individual I have ever played with," Smith said. "He was the heart and soul of our team. From a physical standpoint, there is no one who could match his talent and skill."

Smith is also a huge fan of Aikman. "His leadership and focus are what made us the team we were in the 1990s," Smith said.

Quoted in Tim Durr, "The Life and Career of WR Michael Irvin," Pro Football History, January 29, 2021. www.profootballhistory.com.

Quoted in Pro Football Hall of Fame, "Notes and Quotes on the Class of 2006," January 1, 2005. www.profootballhof.com.

the second game against the Atlanta Falcons. Aikman dropped back and rifled a perfect pass to Irvin, who cut inside at midfield, caught the ball, and raced into the end zone. The 65-yard play was the first touchdown pass of Aikman's professional career.

In 1990, the Cowboys improved to 7–9. They were not yet a playoff team, but Aikman and Irvin were developing chemistry that would lead to greatness in the years to come. An early season game against the Tampa Bay Buccaneers offered a preview. With only 23 seconds left on the clock, Aikman threw a long pass into the end zone, and Irvin caught it for a 28-yard, game-winning touchdown. Later in the season, the quarterback launched a deep ball down the left sideline against the Los Angeles Rams. Irvin was covered, but the speedy receiver made a sudden move and eluded a Rams defender to make the catch. Then he sprinted into the end zone for a 61-yard scoring pass in a 24–21 win. The play showed the confidence Aikman had in his star receiver to win a contested battle for the ball against a defensive back. The deep sideline jump balls became a major part of the duo's great success in future seasons.

The young Cowboys stamped themselves as title contenders during the 1991 season, going 11–5 in the regular season and winning a wild card playoff game. Irvin led the NFL with 1,523 receiving yards in 1991, helping Aikman improve his quarterback rating by 20 points from the previous season. This winning combination turned that potential into the sport's ultimate accomplishment in 1992. In the third game of the season, during a 31–20 win over the Phoenix Cardinals, Aikman and Irvin put on a dazzling show. In the first quarter alone, Irvin caught 87-yard and 41-yard passes for touchdowns. The receiver finished the game with eight catches for a career-high 210 yards and three touchdowns. Aikman completed fourteen of twenty-one passes and amassed 263 yards passing.

After a 13–3 regular season, the Cowboys set their sights on greater accomplishments. On January 10, 1993, they hosted the Philadelphia Eagles in a divisional playoff game at Texas Stadium. While the defense held the Eagles offense to only 178 total yards and sacked Eagles quarterback Randall Cunningham five times, Aikman threw two touchdown passes and finished with 200 yards passing. For his part, Irvin snagged six passes for a game-high 88 yards. A week later, in the NFC title game in San Francisco, Aikman was even better. The quarterback completed twenty-four of thirty-four passes for 322 yards and two touchdowns with no interceptions in a 30–20 victory over the 49ers. Irvin caught six of those passes for 86 yards.

Super Bowl Superstars

The postseason performances of the Cowboys' two superstars, however, were just a prelude for the spectacular Super Bowl XXVII show. The Cowboys led the Buffalo Bills 14–10 late in the second quarter. A touchdown by the Bills would put them in the lead before halftime. Instead, Aikman connected with Irvin for a 19-yard score, delivering a perfect pass to the receiver in the middle of the field. After their kickoff return in the third quarter, the Bills fumbled on their first play from scrimmage, and the Cowboys recovered the ball. With only seconds left in the half, the Cowboys stayed aggressive and shocked the Bills defense with an 18-yard touchdown pass from Aikman to Irvin. Later, Irvin explained how he took advantage of the single defender covering him: "I'd come to the sideline and told a coach, 'They're one-on-one with me,'" Irvin said. "So, I faked him inside and went out."[17]

Once Dallas had climbed the NFL mountain, the team decided it liked the view and stayed on top during the 1993 season. Aikman completed a league-leading 69.1 percent of his pass attempts. Irvin caught eighty-eight passes for 1,330 yards and seven touchdowns during Dallas's 12–4 regular season. The Aikman–Irvin connection continued to dominate in a divisional playoff game, as Irvin caught nine passes for 126 yards and a touchdown in a 27–17 win over Green Bay. Aikman completed twenty-eight of thirty-seven passes

In Super Bowl XXVII, Irvin scores a touchdown thanks to a perfect 19-yard pass from Aikman across the middle of the field. This would be their first Super Bowl win together.

A Scary Ending for the Cowboys' Combo

The Aikman–Irvin passing combo is certainly one of the best in NFL history. Their partnership rose from humble beginnings, a 1–15 season during their first year together, to three-time Super Bowl heroics. However, their on-field relationship ended not in glory but in a terrifying incident during a game against the Eagles in Philadelphia.

On October 10, 1999, as he had so many times before, Aikman completed a pass to Irvin. However, the 8-yard slant pass would be the final play of Irvin's Hall of Fame career. After making a leaping catch, the receiver lowered his head to avoid a collision. The defender's forward motion drove him into Irvin's back, pushing Irvin headfirst into the field's hard surface. The Eagles players involved in the play got up. Irvin did not.

Irvin was motionless for nearly 20 minutes as medical personnel attended to him. Testing later showed that Irvin had been born with a narrow spinal cord, which left him more vulnerable to back injuries than other players. He decided it was too dangerous for him to continue playing football. When Irvin announced his retirement, the Cowboys legend put his usual positive spin on the situation, saying, "Walking away from the game is hard, but *walking* away is a blessing."

Quoted in ABC News, "Injury Forces Irvin to Retire," July 11, 2000. https://abcnews.go.com.

for 302 yards and three touchdowns. Dallas repeated its NFC title game and Super Bowl victories over San Francisco and Buffalo to repeat as NFL champions.

Aikman and Irvin enjoyed strong seasons in 1994, though the Cowboys fell just short of returning to the Super Bowl. After a 12–4 regular season, the Cowboys dismantled the Packers 35–9 in a divisional playoff. Aikman's passing was nearly flawless, and Irvin caught six passes for a team-high 111 yards. The Cowboys were defeated 38–28 by the 49ers in the NFC title game, though the Aikman–Irvin connection was as brilliant as ever. The duo teamed up twelve times for 192 yards and two touchdowns.

The Last Roundups

The Cowboys rode off into the sunset with another title after the 1995 season. After another 12–4 regular season, the Cowboys dispatched the Eagles, the Packers, and the Steelers. Aikman compiled one-hundred-plus passer ratings in all three games. Irvin followed up his NFC title game performance with five catches for 76 yards during the 27–17 win over the Steelers in Super Bowl XXX.

While neither player would return to the Super Bowl, Aikman and Irvin showed they still had the magic during the 1996 season. The duo defeated Miami, then coached by their former mentor Jimmy Johnson, in a 29–10 victory. Aikman threw for 363 yards and three touchdowns, with Irvin hauling in twelve passes for 186 yards and a score. Later in the season, the duo dominated Arizona thanks to Irvin, who finished with eight catches for 198 yards and a touchdown. In a wild card playoff game, Irvin totaled 103 yards on eight catches during a 40–15 rout of Minnesota. Although Dallas lost in the divisional round to Carolina 26–17, the team had remained dominant from 1991 to 1998. Only an injury to Irvin early in the 1999 season brought a premature end to its success.

"I have great rapport with Troy. I have a serious, serious man-to-man love for him. I want to make plays for him."[18]

—Michael Irvin, former Cowboys receiver

During Dallas's dynasty, the team's top receiver and quarterback developed a special bond. "I have great rapport with Troy," Irvin said in a 1997 interview. "I have a serious, serious man-to-man love for him. I want to make plays for him. I want him to be confident in me. To know I want to win."[18] Aikman appreciated having a receiver who was so confident and would compete so hard. "He'd draw coverage, of course, there'd be two, sometimes three guys, on him," Aikman said in a 2023 interview. "The guys called me Roy. He'd say 'Roy, you gotta throw it up to me, give me a chance!' I said, 'Michael, I'm not throwing it into triple coverage.' But . . . like all of . . . the great ones, they always feel like they have a chance. That's what makes them great."[19]

Colts Connection: Peyton Manning and Marvin Harrison

Peyton Manning and Marvin Harrison had exceptional rapport from the start. "The very first preseason game, my very first pass, I threw a five-yard pass, and Marvin Harrison ran 48 yards for a touchdown," Manning said. "I remember thinking, 'The NFL is easy. You just throw a short pass, and Marvin Harrison will run for touchdowns.' Which is pretty much what he did for the entire time we played together. I don't believe that record that me and Marvin have of throwing the most touchdowns together will ever be broken."[20]

> "I don't believe that record that me and Marvin have of throwing the most touchdowns together will ever be broken."[20]
>
> —Peyton Manning, former Colts quarterback

Indianapolis Colts teammates from 1998 to 2008, Manning and Harrison blended athletic ability with keen intelligence and a strong work ethic to put up record-breaking numbers. They combined for regular season records in completions (953), yards (12,766), and touchdowns (112). Manning, one of the greatest quarterbacks to ever play the game, worked as hard off the field as on. He had the outstanding ability to read defenses, make quick decisions, and deliver the ball with pinpoint accuracy. The six-foot-five, 230-pound quarterback set numerous records in his career, with the precise route-running Harrison the major reason. "The greatest thing about Marvin's routes," Manning said, "was that the first five-to-seven yards all looked exactly the same. They couldn't tell if it was a five-yard slant, a 10-yard out, a 12-yard hook, or a 40-yard take off. They were always afraid he was going to go deep. He was truly one of a kind."[21]

Young Colts Stars Buck Up

Once one of the premier teams in the NFL, the Colts organization had struggled for decades to field a winning team. Founded in Maryland as the Baltimore Colts in 1953, the team's high-water mark was its 1970 victory in Super Bowl V behind the play of steely quarterback Johnny Unitas.

In 1984, Baltimore officials threatened to seize the team over a stadium dispute with Colts owner Robert Irsay, who packed up the franchise in the middle of the night and moved it to Indiana. Despite the change of scenery, the team's fortunes did not improve until the 1996 and 1998 NFL drafts. In 1996 the Colts drafted Harrison, a speedy, six-foot, 185-pound receiver, in hopes of improving their offensive attack. That picture was not complete until the Colts chose Manning with the first overall pick in 1998.

> **"The greatest thing about Marvin's routes was that the first five-to-seven yards all looked exactly the same. They couldn't tell if it was a five-yard slant, a 10-yard out, a 12-yard hook, or a 40-yard take off."[21]**
>
> —Peyton Manning, former Colts quarterback

It took a full season before the rookie quarterback and young receiver really showed what they could do. The first real glimmer of the talented duo showed up during a road game in San Francisco on October 18, 1998. Harrison caught three touchdown passes from Manning, the last a 61-yarder in the third quarter. The Colts threw a major scare into the talented 49ers before falling 34–31. Five weeks later, Harrison caught nine passes for 128 yards and a touchdown from Manning as the Colts got their second win of the year, 24–23 over the New York Jets.

Manning (left) and Harrison watch from the sidelines during a game in 2003. Teammates from 1998 to 2008, the pair put up record-breaking numbers.

The Colts reversed their record during the second year of the Manning–Harrison era, going 13–3 in 1999. The two young stars showed how quickly they were becoming a serious threat to opposing defenses when they went up against the San Diego Chargers at the beginning of the new season. Harrison caught thirteen passes for a career-high 196 yards and a touchdown. Manning finished with a new Colts passing record of 404 yards.

Clearly, something special was developing between Manning and Harrison. They were showing an ability to improvise and make big plays in difficult situations, a skill that usually takes a passing combination several years to develop. After overwhelming the Chargers secondary, Harrison was confident he and his quarterback would enjoy many more outstanding days together. "I'm happy we're winning," the receiver said after the game. "If it takes Peyton and me to do what we did today, then that's what we'll keep doing."[22]

A Great First Impression

As in any relationship, finding common ground and connection can take time, but Marvin Harrison quickly realized there was great potential in his relationship with Peyton Manning. "I didn't know anything about Peyton," Harrison recalled. "But the first day of practice, I saw the determination on his face and the way he was on the field. I said, 'He wants to be good!' He was ready to do what he had to do to get that team where it needed to be."

The third-year receiver's perception of the rookie quarterback was spot-on. Manning and Harrison became the most prolific quarterback-receiver combination in NFL history. But it did not happen because of talent alone, though both players possessed that in abundance. It took an incredible amount of work by both players, constantly trying to get better no matter how much they had achieved. Their mutual respect for each other's work ethic lasted all eleven seasons that they played together. "He practices as hard as he can every single day," Manning said of Harrison. "It's a real credit to him. He's always been a great professional that way."

Stephen Holder, "Marvin Harrison's Work Ethic Rewarded," IndyStar, February 7, 2016. www.indystar.com.

Quoted in Colts.com, "Peyton Manning Quotes," November 11, 2008. www.colts.com.

Colts Stampede

Indeed, the teammates would go where no passing combos had gone before, and the Colts would keep winning. The Colts won a respectable ten games in each of the following nine seasons except one, and Manning won three of his record five MVPs playing with Harrison. Harrison caught at least ten touchdown passes every year from 1999 to 2006 and topped 1,000 receiving yards in all eight of those seasons.

The two stars worked tirelessly to improve themselves. Both spent hours watching the film of each previous game in preparation for the next. They and their teammates also lifted weights to strengthen their bodies. On the field, practice drills also helped the team cohere as a unit, with Harrison and Manning often the last players to call it quits for the day. Their extra efforts helped them grow together and bring out the best in each other. "We went through the bumps and bruises," Harrison said. "But we've developed a rapport where we can do things without speaking."[23]

> **"We went through the bumps and bruises. But we've developed a rapport where we can do things without speaking."[23]**
>
> —Marvin Harrison, former Colts receiver

One example of how explosive the Manning–Harrison combination could be occurred during the so-called Monday Night Miracle in 2003, when Indianapolis became the first team in NFL history to rally from 21 points down inside of 4 minutes to win. Trailing defending Super Bowl champion Tampa Bay, which boasted one of the most talented defenses in NFL history, Indianapolis scored to cut its deficit to 35–21. Then Manning hit Harrison with a 28-yard touchdown pass on fourth down to make it 35–28 with 2:29 remaining. When Indianapolis got the ball back, Manning connected with Harrison for 52 yards, and Ricky Williams scored the tying touchdown on a 1-yard run with 35 seconds left.

Manning passes during the Monday Night Miracle in 2003. Powered by the Manning-Harrison combination, the Colts overcame a 21-point deficit with four minutes remaining to win 38–35.

Beating the Best

Peyton Manning and Marvin Harrison enjoyed some of their best moments against the best players and teams. Even Deion Sanders, considered the greatest cover cornerback ever, fell victim to a 40-yard touchdown pass from Manning to Harrison during Indianapolis's 34–24 win over Dallas in 1999. Sanders was fooled by Manning, thinking the play was a run, and Harrison streaked past him. "I looked back there and Marvin ran a deep post for six," Sanders recalled. "It looked like it was the (fault of) safety because it was in the middle of the field. The coach blasted the safety when we got back to the sideline. I said, 'No, that was me.'"

In 2006, Indianapolis faced nemesis New England, coached by Bill Belichick, often called the greatest defensive mind in NFL history. In a 27–20 road win, Harrison made what his coach, Tony Dungy, called likely the greatest catch of the receiver's career. "Back shoulder fade, a little bit to his left and the one hand, tip it back to yourself, drag both feet in the end zone," Dungy said. "That to me was the masterpiece catch." Harrison caught eight passes from Manning during the game for 145 yards and two touchdowns.

Quoted in Stephen Holder, "That Time Marvin Harrison Dusted Deion Sanders," IndyStar, February 4, 2016. www.indystar.com.

Quoted in Kevin Bowen, "Peyton Manning on Marvin Harrison: 'He Truly Was One of a Kind,'" Colts.com, August 6, 2016. www.colts.com.

Indianapolis won 38–35 in overtime, thanks to the team's incredibly productive passing partners. Manning threw for 386 yards, and Harrison caught eleven passes for 176 yards and two touchdowns.

Manning has called the incredible comeback one of the favorite games of his illustrious career. He knew there was one player he could keep throwing to who was capable of making enough big plays to get the Colts back in the game: "In the second half, we just said, 'Let's go. Let's just go with it. If they play two (deep), I'll hit Marvin. If they play one (deep), I'll work the outside. I don't care who's out there (covering) Marvin. I really don't.'"[24]

Taking It to Another Level

The 2004 season kept the Manning–Harrison train rolling. That year, Manning set a record by throwing forty-nine touchdown passes on his way to winning his second consecutive MVP. Harrison tied his career high with fifteen touchdown catches that season. The receiver also matched his career single-game best by catching three of Manning's six touchdown passes, totaling game highs with twelve catches for 127 yards, during a 41–9 Thanksgiving Day feasting on the Detroit Lions.

In 2005, the duo connected for some special moments. In the fourth quarter of a Monday night home game against the St. Louis Rams, Manning lofted a perfect pass to the right corner of the end zone. Harrison caught the ball only inches from the out-of-bounds marker for the touchdown. The 6-yard score set the record for most touchdowns for a quarterback-receiver combination, and the Colts won 45-28. The two superstars, always so efficient when playing the game, were a bit confused as to what to do with the record-breaking football. "He had it, he gave it to me, I gave it back to him and he gave it back to me," Manning said. "We're going to try to cut it in half, that's the way it should be."[25]

The record-setting season continued when, on November 7, 2005, the Colts brought their 7–0 record to New England. The Patriots had knocked the Colts out of the playoffs the previous two seasons on their way to winning Super Bowls. But Manning and Harrison made sure there would not be another crushing loss on this Monday night, connecting nine times for a game-high 128 yards in a 40–21 victory. The duo started it with a first-quarter touchdown pass for the first points of the game and finished it with a 30-yard fourth-quarter score.

Winning Ways

The Colts' winning ways continued as the playoffs approached. On November 28, in a Monday night home game against the Steelers, the pair showed an aggressive, quick-strike ability. On the Colts' first offensive play of the game, Manning threw a deep ball to Harrison, who had gotten well behind the Steelers secondary. Harrison caught the perfect pass near the right sideline and easily ran into the end zone. The big play propelled the Colts to a 26–7 win and a 14–2 regular season. However, they suffered a heartbreaking 21–18 home loss to the eventual Super Bowl champion Steelers in a divisional playoff game.

Accustomed to losses, fans and the media alike openly wondered whether the Colts, despite all of Manning's and Harrison's heroics, would ever win the Super Bowl. The team's successful regular-season play just did not seem to carry into the playoffs. That scenario finally changed in 2006. After a stellar 12–4 regular season, the Colts defeated the Chiefs, the Ravens, and the Patriots in the playoffs. For the first time in thirty-six years, the Colts were headed to the Super Bowl.

On February 4, 2007, a rainy Miami Sunday, the Colts faced the Chicago Bears in Super Bowl XLI. The Bears struck first, with Devin Hester returning the opening kickoff for a touchdown. The Colts offense, meanwhile, got off to a slow start, with Manning throwing an interception on their first drive. On their next drive, Manning threw a 53-yard touchdown pass to receiver Reggie Wayne. Yet by the end of the first quarter, the Colts trailed 14–6. But early in the second quarter, a tight pass to Harrison got the Colts offense chugging once again. For the next three quarters, the Colts overwhelmed their opponents and won the game 29–17. Manning passed for 247 yards and one touchdown and was named Super Bowl MVP. Harrison contributed five receptions for 59 yards as he and his quarterback added a Super Bowl ring, the one thing that had eluded them, to their exceptional list of accomplishments.

Patriots Prestige: Tom Brady and Rob Gronkowski

When rookie tight end Rob Gronkowski got to the NFL, he learned that football was not only a game but a business as well. That lesson came from Tom Brady, already a superstar quarterback, in 2010. "I'm like, this isn't anything like 'Any Given Sunday,'" Gronkowski said, referring to a movie about pro football. "This guy [Brady] is yelling at me if I mess up a tad bit. This guy is yelling at me like a coach. . . . It took me a bit to realize where it was coming from. . . . He was kind of hard on me at first because I think he saw some talent in me and the opportunity that was presented in front of me."[26]

> "This guy [Brady] is yelling at me if I mess up a tad bit. This guy is yelling at me like a coach. . . . He was kind of hard on me at first because I think he saw some talent in me."[26]
>
> —Rob Gronkowski, former NFL tight end

After that rocky start, the Brady–Gronkowski tandem would go on to wreak havoc with NFL defenses over the next ten-plus years, first with New England and later with Tampa Bay. They were teammates on three Super Bowl–winning New England teams and another with Tampa Bay.

Great Players Who Are Greater Together

Brady, with seven Super Bowl titles, is among the greatest NFL quarterbacks. Picked as the 199th overall selection during the 2000 NFL draft, Brady exhibited laser-like accuracy as a passer, along with keen intelligence on the field. Over twenty-seven seasons, the six-foot-four, 225-pound quarterback notched NFL records in all major passing categories and won a record five Super Bowl MVP awards.

And while Brady clicked with many receivers over his career, Gronkowski was his favorite target. Known to teammates and fans as "Gronk," the tight end provided a rare combination of size (six foot six, 265 pounds), strength, and speed. Over eleven seasons together, Brady and Gronkowski scored ninety-three regular-season touchdowns and a then-record fifteen postseason scores. Gronkowski surpassed 1,000 yards receiving in four seasons and added 1,389 postseason yards.

The Patriots drafted Gronkowski in 2010, and during the first few games the tight end got off to a slow start. The pair's inauspicious beginning is evidenced by Gronkowski's recollection of a 2010 team film session. "[Brady] is like 'Get outside. You've got to get outside of the defender,'" Gronkowski said. "I wasn't really that athletic as a rookie. I couldn't get outside, and Brady just turns around in the meeting because it was on film and he goes 'Gronk, I'm . . . done throwing you the ball.' . . . That fired me up. I was like 'Oh, I'm gonna show this guy.' But that's the leadership he had. He was brutally honest, and he would get you to the next level."[27]

Practice Makes Patriots Stars Near Perfect

The two future Hall of Famers first got in tune during a November 14, 2010, game against the Pittsburgh Steelers. That game suggested theirs could be a match made in football heaven. In the late season matchup, Gronkowski caught three touchdown passes from Brady in a 39–26 win over the Steelers. Now, for the first time in his career, Brady had a reliable target, and the tight end proved that he could do what few had done before him.

Brady saw the talent Gronkowski had and made sure the rookie learned how to do things the right way. "Every single day after practice, he would make me stay," Gronkowski said. "He would

Tom Brady (left) talks with Rob Gronkowski during the New England training camp in 2011. The pair would go on to wreak havoc with NFL defenses over the next ten years.

make like two other rookies stay, and he'd be like, 'We're getting on the same page.' And he'd be throwing pass after pass, route after route."[28]

Things really clicked between the two in 2011. Brady threw for 5,235 yards and thirty-nine touchdowns. Gronkowski caught ninety passes for 1,327 yards. On January 14, 2012, in a divisional playoff, Brady threw for 363 yards and six touchdowns in a 45–10 demolition of Denver. Gronkowski caught three of the touchdowns, all before halftime. A week later, New England met Baltimore in the AFC Championship Game and eked out a tough 23–20 win—sending them to the Super Bowl.

> **"Every single day after practice, [Brady] would make me stay. . . . He'd be like, 'We're getting on the same page.' And he'd be throwing pass after pass, route after route."[28]**
>
> —Rob Gronkowski, former NFL tight end

Following His Friend's Footsteps to Florida

Rob Gronkowski retired from the NFL after the 2018 season at the age of twenty-nine. The New England tight end had dominated NFL defenses since coming into the league in 2010, but Gronkowski's fearless attitude and incredibly physical style of play had resulted in many injuries. He decided to call it quits shortly after catching six passes for 87 yards during New England's 13–3 win over the Los Angeles Rams in Super Bowl LIII in February 2019. However, his retirement lasted only thirteen months. Gronkowski joined the Tampa Bay Buccaneers in April 2020, not long after former New England quarterback Tom Brady signed with the team.

"We have great chemistry out there and every time we get together, it's just like the old days," Gronkowski said of his decision to join his friend in Florida. "It just happened to be the right opportunity, down in Tampa. Tom is like the appetizer of the whole meal. He got me hooked when he went down to Tampa."

Quoted in Christopher Price, "Rob Gronkowski Explains Why He Came Out of Retirement and How He Ended Up with the Buccaneers," Boston.com, April 22, 2020. www.boston.com.

Super Bowl XLVI, held on February 5, 2012, was the first to be played in Indiana and pitted the Patriots against the New York Giants. Both teams were looking to win their fourth Super Bowl, and the Patriots went into the big game as favorites, despite having been beaten by the Giants in the regular season. In the first half, the Giants jumped out to an early 9–0 lead before the Patriots came roaring back with 17 unanswered points. Giants quarterback Eli Manning threw for 296 yards and was nearly matched by Brady's 276 yards, but by the second half, the Giants defense held tough. A 6-yard running touchdown by Giants back Ahmad Bradshaw with 57 seconds left in the game proved to be the difference, as the Giants beat the Patriots 21–17.

Back to the Big Game

After earning a 12–4 record during the 2014 season, the Patriots were once again in the hunt for a world championship. They racked up convincing playoff wins against the Ravens and the Colts, scoring more than 30 points in each game. Now they were set to meet the Seattle Seahawks in Super Bowl XLIX on February 1, 2015.

The game marked the Patriots' eighth trip to the Super Bowl, a record matched only by the Pittsburgh Steelers and Dallas Cowboys. The Seahawks, meanwhile, boasted a Super Bowl win the previous year, a 12–4 regular-season record, and one of the toughest pass defenses in the NFL. Known to Seahawks fans as the Legion of Boom, their All-Pro secondary seemed certain to keep a lid on Brady and Gronkowski's high-scoring offense.

The game's first quarter yielded no points for either team, with Brady throwing an early interception on the Seattle 10-yard line. New England forced Seattle to punt at the start of the second quarter, after which Brady's offense marched 65 yards down the field. With 31 seconds left in the half, Brady found Gronkowski for a 22-yard touchdown pass. The score was tied 14–14.

Brady throws a pass during the first half of Super Bowl XLIX against the Seattle Seahawks. The game marked the Patriots' eighth trip to the Super Bowl.

Football Finished but Friends Forever

Theirs appeared to be an unlikely friendship. Rob Gronkowski's persona implied a devil-may-care attitude, a lovable goofball who just happened to have rare football ability. Tom Brady was all business all the time, the sixth-round draft pick who proved everyone wrong with an unsurpassed level of determination. But while Brady and Gronkowski showed their obvious chemistry on the field, they also enjoyed a tremendous friendship away from the game.

"He's one of the most unique people," Brady said of Gronkowski. "Just being around him, he's so positive. I think everybody wishes in their next life they come back as Rob just because he's got such a great personality."

When Gronkowski retired for good after the 2021 season at thirty-three, he shared a Brady–Gronkowski highlight video to the sound of Queen's "You're My Best Friend." Gronkowski wrote in the post, "Tommy Boy!!! This football journey with you has been nothing short of special. Thank you for your dedication to the game, putting the team in the best possible position to win every year, all the records that were broken, the Super Bowls, the memories, and your friendship through the last 12 years."

Quoted in Justin Leger, "Brady Opens Up About His Close Relationship with Gronk," NBC Sports Boston, February 4, 2021. www.nbcsportsboston.com.

Quoted in Paulina Dedaj, "Rob Gronkowski Thanks Tom Brady with Heartfelt Message: 'You're a Legend and Always Will Be,'" Fox News, February 2, 2022. ww.foxnews.com.

During the third quarter, Seattle pounced, scoring 10 more points to take the lead, 24–14. Heading into the final 12 minutes of the game, New England's chances looked grim, until two late touchdowns put the team ahead for a 28–24 win. Although Brady tossed two interceptions in the game, he threw for 328 yards and four touchdowns. Gronkowski only caught one touchdown pass during that game, but his versatility allowed New England to use him in a variety of ways. He could stand on the line of scrimmage and be a devastating blocker, or he could slip away from a defender for short but crucial pass completions. And because of his size and speed, defenders trying to cover him one-on-one barely stood a chance when he ran along the sideline.

Brady's ability to get the ball out quickly and his amazing understanding of NFL defenses enabled him to put the ball in places where only Gronkowski could catch it. The pair was especially effective near the goal line. Brady would often lob the ball high in the air, knowing Gronkowski was likely to come down with it in the end zone. Gronkowski also possessed the speed to run deep routes, and Brady was an extremely accurate deep-ball thrower.

Difficult Defeats and Wonderful Wins

The Patriots' successful 2015 season seemed destined for glory, but it was not to be. They finished one game short of the Super Bowl, falling to the Broncos 20–18 during the AFC Championship Game in January 2016. It was not for lack of trying that the Patriots lost. Brady and Gronkowski connected eight times for 144 yards and a 4-yard touchdown that pulled the Patriots within two points with just 12 seconds left.

The following season the Patriots pushed themselves harder and further, reaching Super Bowl LI. They overcame a 28–3 second-half deficit to beat the Atlanta Falcons 34–28 in overtime. But they did so without their star tight end, who missed the epic comeback, and much of the season, because of injury.

But Gronkowski was back in top form in 2017. During a December 17 game against the Steelers, Gronkowski caught nine passes from Brady for a career-high 168 yards in a 27–24 win. On Christmas Eve, Gronkowski combined with Brady on one of their most spectacular plays. In the second quarter of a 37–16 win over the Buffalo Bills, the Patriots had the ball at the Bills 17-yard line. Brady tossed a beautiful pass along the left sideline, and Gronkowski made a dazzling one-handed catch over a stunned Bills defender for a touchdown.

Gronkowski later talked about the relationship the two developed on and off the field. "I would say basically the friendships are developed over football too," Gronkowski said. "Over studying football together, getting together in the offseason, extra stuff during the season and you just want to build that up so you can be on the same page."[29]

Retirement After Reaching the Top

After more than a decade of catching Tom Brady's passes, Gronkowski retired after the 2018 season. Few, if any, quarterback-receiver tandems had been as successful. And while Brady played one more year in New England, his days with the Patriots, who looked to revitalize their team, were numbered. In March 2020, Brady joined the Tampa Bay Buccaneers. Gronkowski came out of retirement to join him in Florida. Together again, they did what they do best. Brady threw forty touchdown passes in 2020 and led the league in 2021 with 5,316 yards and forty-three touchdown throws. Gronkowski caught thirteen touchdown passes in those two seasons. Brady was named Super Bowl LV's MVP after throwing three touchdown passes during Tampa Bay's 31–9 thumping of Kansas City in February 2021. Gronkowski caught two touchdown passes and also led his team in catches.

> **"It's been amazing to watch him perform. He's obviously the greatest tight end to ever play the game."[30]**
>
> —Tom Brady, former NFL quarterback

Gronkowski retired again after the 2021 season, and Brady followed the next year. Later, Brady remembered the tight end as one of the best. "It's been amazing to watch him perform," Brady said. "He's obviously the greatest tight end to ever play the game. I think his ability to block in the run game, run routes in the pass game, win against smaller players, and then he's very clutch. He comes up big in the biggest moments."[30]

Gronkowski, meanwhile, remembered his seasons with Brady with fondness and admiration. "It's a lot of fun," Gronkowski said. "The guy is just so precise with everything. Just the way he is out on the field, the way he prepares, the way he goes into these games. You know every single time, you're going to get the best out of him no matter what the situations are, and that's what's so great about playing with him. It makes football the best it can possibly be."[31]

CHAPTER SIX

Hail to the Chiefs: Patrick Mahomes and Travis Kelce

During the 2023 NFL season, Travis Kelce was part of two superstar duos. Kelce's relationship with singer-songwriter megastar Taylor Swift grabbed headlines around the world and resulted in a new group of fans—Swift's admirers, known as "Swifties"—tuning in to Kansas City Chiefs games. But it was on the field, pairing with his sensational quarterback Patrick Mahomes, that the tight end cemented his place in history. "He's the best receiving tight end to ever play the game,"[32] says Rob Gronkowski, considered by many to be one of the NFL's best tight ends.

> **"[Kelce]'s the best receiving tight end to ever play the game."[32]**
>
> —Rob Gronkowski, former NFL tight end

As Gronkowski well understands, tight ends are only as good as their quarterbacks. And like Gronkowski, Kelce has played with one of the sport's top quarterbacks. Kansas City Chiefs quarterback Patrick Mahomes is off to the best start to a career of any quarterback in NFL history. Since Mahomes became the starter in 2018, Kansas City has won at least eleven of seventeen games every season.

For Kansas City, the chemistry between Mahomes and Kelce takes the team's scoring potential and dominance to another level. "We think along the same wavelengths," Mahomes said. "There might be something that we haven't talked about

"We think along the same wavelengths. There might be something that we haven't talked about that he does, and I just know he's going to do it."[33]

—Patrick Mahomes, Chiefs quarterback

that he does, and I just know he's going to do it."[33] Kelce combines top-notch athleticism with an uncanny knack for finding an open spot, often in the middle of several defenders. He has excellent hands and is extremely difficult to tackle after making a catch because of his size and speed. Mahomes has all the tools and intangibles anyone would want in a quarterback: tremendous arm strength and accuracy, terrific mobility, crucial intelligence, extraordinary creativity, and a fierce desire to win. The two players have led Kansas City to three Super Bowl wins: in 2020, 2023, and 2024.

Great Draft Picks Lead to a Great Combo

Dynasties in the NFL are built on teamwork, coaching, and the high-level skills and talents of players. The Kansas City Chiefs, founded as the Dallas Texans in 1959, became a contender almost from the outset, especially after their move to Kansas City, Missouri, in 1963. They won championships in 1962, 1966, and 1969, and defeated the Minnesota Vikings 23-7 in Super Bowl IV on January 11, 1970. Yet the team faltered through most of the next five decades. It was not until Patrick Mahomes became the Chiefs starter in 2018 that the magic finally returned to Kansas City.

That year, the duo of Mahomes and Kelce emerged as a force on the football field. Mahomes, at six foot two and 225 pounds, was league MVP, throwing for 5,097 yards and an NFL-leading fifty touchdowns. Kelce, at six foot five and 250 pounds, set career highs with 103 catches for 1,336 yards and ten touchdowns. The two showed their vast potential in a 40–33 win over the Raiders on December 2, connecting twelve times for 168 yards and two scores. During one notable play, with the Chiefs on the Raiders 6-yard line, Mahomes took the snap, rolled to his right, and fired a pass toward Kelce, who made the shoestring catch in the end zone. Yet even plays like that were not enough to propel the Chiefs to the Super Bowl that year.

The 2019 season was different. The Chiefs finished the regular season with a record of 12–4, but Mahomes and Kelce had saved their best moments for the postseason. In a divisional playoff game against the Houston Texans, the Chiefs trailed 24–0 in the second quarter. That situation would seem hopeless for other teams. But other teams do not have Mahomes and Kelce. Kelce caught three touchdown passes from Mahomes as the Chiefs roared back to take a 28–24 halftime lead. Mahomes threw five touchdown passes, and Kelce finished with a game-high ten receptions in a 51–31 victory.

The Chiefs went on to win the AFC Championship Game, leading to a February 2020 Super Bowl match against the San Francisco 49ers. The Chiefs trailed 20–10 in the fourth quarter, but a Mahomes to Kelce touchdown pass cut the deficit to 20–17 with just over 6 minutes left in the game. This was followed by a touchdown pass to back Damien Williams, which put the Chiefs in front just before the 2-minute warning. Another touchdown and an interception of a 49ers pass sealed a 31–20 victory. Mahomes

The Chiefs' Travis Kelce is hugged by girlfriend Taylor Swift after winning the NFL's AFC Championship game in 2025. Kelce is considered to be one of the best tight ends ever.

won Super Bowl MVP, and Kelce contributed six catches. It was the Chiefs' first Super Bowl win in fifty years.

Mahomes and Kelce picked up where they'd left off in the 2020 season. Mahomes threw for 4,740 yards and thirty-eight touchdowns. He was only intercepted six times. Kelce set a season record for tight ends with 1,416 yards receiving. He achieved career highs in receptions (105) and touchdown catches (11). The tandem excelled again in the postseason, connecting for three touchdowns as the Chiefs won two playoff games before losing to the Tampa Bay Buccaneers in Super Bowl LV in February 2021.

Huge Fans of Each Other

During the 2020 season, the quarterback-receiver duo talked about what made their partnership so successful. "His understanding of coverages and how he runs routes is special," Mahomes said of Kelce. "I think that's the best thing about his game.

Besting the Bills

Patrick Mahomes and Travis Kelce share an almost mystical ability to make the biggest plays in the most pressure-packed situations. The Buffalo Bills know this all too well. With 8 seconds left in regulation play during the AFC divisional playoff game in January 2022, the Chiefs had the ball on their own 44-yard line, but they were trailing the Bills 36–33. The situation seemed nearly hopeless, but Kelce paused, sized up the defense, and told Mahomes he could exploit a gap in the Bills' pass coverage to gain some vital yards. The quarterback responded, "Do it, Kels. Do it, do it, Kels."

On the next play, Kelce sprinted down the middle of the field and found an open area between his two defenders. Mahomes's pass hit him perfectly in stride, and the tight end rumbled to the Bills 31-yard line to set up the game-tying field goal. Then the Chiefs marched to the winning touchdown in overtime. From the Bills 8-yard line, Mahomes floated a pass to the right side of the end zone. Kelce turned at the precise moment, made the catch, and got both feet in bounds for a 42–36 win in one of the wildest playoff games in NFL history.

Quoted in Nate Chute, "What Did Travis Kelce Say to Patrick Mahomes During Game-Tying, 13-Second Drive vs. the Bills?," *Lubbock (TX) Avalanche-Journal*, January 25, 2022. www.lubbockonline.com.

Patrick Mahomes throws a pass in a game during the 2018 season. It was just his first year as a starter, but he went on to throw for 5,097 yards and was named league MVP.

Obviously, he's physically gifted and he's a mismatch for guys on the field—linebackers, corners, whoever it is."[34] Kelce conveyed an equal appreciation of his quarterback. "Obviously, I'm a big fan of Pat's," Kelce said. "I think he's the best player in the [NFL]. . . . When Pat got into the huddle, it was just a little bit different. He brought a different energy, different style to the game that even I was a little more accustomed to, just going out and playing ball in the backyard type of football."[35]

> **"Obviously, I'm a big fan of Pat's. I think he's the best player in the [NFL]."[35]**
>
> —Travis Kelce, Chiefs tight end

In 2021, Mahomes and Kelce continued their league dominance. Mahomes's knack for eluding defenders, throwing on

Friendship Extends Beyond the Football Field

On the field, Patrick Mahomes and Travis Kelce enjoy an unsurpassed connection. Off the field, the Kansas City quarterback and tight end have formed a lasting friendship. Mahomes and Kelce have traveled, golfed, starred in commercials, and opened a restaurant together. Their appreciation for their friendship is clear in how they describe each other.

"He makes every person feel like they're the most important person in the world," Mahomes says of Kelce. "He has that natural gift to really embrace and show love to everybody."

Kelce also sees their relationship as special. Mahomes, he says, "is family now. It's something that's genuine, and I'm sure the relationship is going to go far beyond this game."

Quoted in Rachel DeSantis, "NFL BFFs Patrick Mahomes and Travis Kelce 'Can't Even Put Into Words' Their Love for Each Other," *People*, November 24, 2022. https://people.com.

Quoted in Pete Grathoff, "Chiefs' Patrick Mahomes, Travis Kelce Share Genesis of Friendship on 'Today' Show," *For Pete's Sake* (blog), *Kansas City Star*, November 10, 2022. www.kansascity.com.

the run, and sending accurate passes straight into the hands of his receivers made him more dangerous than ever. That season, he threw for 4,839 yards and thirty-seven touchdowns. Kelce, with his uncanny ability to shake cornerbacks, accounted for nearly one-fifth of those yards by catching ninety-two passes for 1,125 yards.

The two stars showed their greatness again during a 34–28 win over the Los Angeles Chargers on December 16. The duo teamed up for a game-tying 7-yard score with just over a minute left in regulation play, then ended the contest with a 34-yard touchdown in overtime. On the winning play, Kelce caught a short pass over the middle and avoided several defenders on his way to the end zone, finishing with a career-best 191 yards receiving. The duo provided more postseason highlights, but the Chiefs did not make the Super Bowl that season.

The next season, however, ended in glory with Kansas City winning Super Bowl LVII in February 2023. Yet it was often the regular season where Mahomes and Kelce found their greatest moments. In an October 2022, game against the Las Vegas Raiders, Kansas City trailed 17–0 in the second quarter. With only 4 minutes left in the first half, Kelce caught a 1-yard pass from Mahomes for a touchdown. With 17 seconds left, Las Vegas added a field goal; then, at the last second, Kansas City kicked a field goal.

Energized by their first-half momentum, the Chiefs fought on. Kelce led the way by eluding tacklers and catching two short touchdown passes, the second of which put the Chiefs ahead by 3 points. One more Kelce touchdown catch from Mahomes in the fourth quarter kept the Chiefs ahead for good. They held on to win the game 30–29. This was neither the first nor last time that the resilience and determination of the two stars led them to glory.

The Chiefs Remain on Top

The Chiefs were again on top of the NFL during the 2023 season. Early on, the Mahomes–Kelce combo connected on twenty-eight consecutive passes over three games.

The duo continued to show top form in the January 2024 AFC Championship Game against the Baltimore Ravens. Kelce caught all eleven passes thrown to him for 116 yards and a touchdown. A 19-yard touchdown pass came on the Chiefs' first drive. Mahomes fired a tight pass near the right sideline, and Kelce outmaneuvered Ravens All-Pro safety Kyle Hamilton to make a difficult catch in the end zone. On the Chiefs' next possession, the quarterback and tight end blended on a play that epitomized the Mahomes–Kelce magic, even if it was only for a 10-yard gain. On a third-and-5 play from the Ravens 27-yard line, Mahomes dropped back but could not find anyone open. The quarterback scrambled but was about to be caught when he tossed a pass at the last moment. Kelce had kept working to get open and made an astonishing diving catch for a first down. The play showed how much Mahomes and Kelce frustrate defenders. Even when opponents play perfect defense, they often cannot stop the Chiefs' combo. Shortly after that highlight-reel play, the Chiefs scored to take a 14–7 lead. The game ended in a 17–10 trip to the Super Bowl for the Chiefs.

No team had repeated as Super Bowl champions since the Patriots after the 2003 and 2004 seasons. The Chiefs needed all of the unrivaled ability, toughness, and determination of their biggest stars to win their second consecutive Super Bowl in February 2024, but by the end of the second quarter, the Chiefs trailed the 49ers 10–0. Then the game turned as Mahomes connected with his top target eight times for 92 yards after halftime. In the second half, the tandem connected on a 22-yard, third-down play in the last half-minute of regulation, leading to a game-tying field goal. With the score now locked at 19–19, the play clock ran out, sending the game into a rare Super Bowl overtime.

After the coin toss went San Francisco's way, its offense marched down the field, deep into Kansas City territory, but the drive ended with a 3-point field goal. As the NFL's overtime rules dictate, the opposing team would also get a chance to score. Kansas City promptly drove 75 yards downfield, mixing runs and passes, before arriving on the San Francisco 10-yard line. Then,

Kelce and Mahomes slap hands during Super Bowl LVIII, which they went on to win in their second super bowl victory. The duo is one of the greatest NFL pairings of all time.

facing a second-and-7, Mahomes hit Kelce with a short pass over the middle for 7 yards. It proved a crucial play, setting up a 3-yard toss from Mahomes to Mecole Hardman Jr. for 6 points and a 25–22 Super Bowl victory.

With another Super Bowl win, the Chiefs staked their claim to being one of the greatest teams of their era—much of it due to the electrifying combination of Mahomes and Kelce. In addition to throwing for 333 yards and two touchdowns, Mahomes led the team with 66 yards rushing in winning his third Super Bowl MVP award. Kelce supplied game bests in catches and yards. "The guys never faltered," Mahomes said. "This is awesome. It's legendary."[36]

The Duo Comes Up Big in Biggest Moments

What is also legendary is the historic level of clutch play by the Mahomes–Kelce duo. The two stars have incredible confidence in each other, especially in pressure situations. Kelce knows if he keeps working and gets open, Mahomes will use his ability to scramble away from pass rushers to keep plays alive and eventually find him. Mahomes often throws to Kelce in tight coverage, knowing the tight end will use his size, strength, and competitive nature to make the catch. "They're always on the same page," former Chiefs receiver Marquez Valdes-Scantling said. "They don't have to look at each other. They can freestyle and not know what each other is going to do and still be on the same page. No matter what you do, you can't defend it."[37]

SOURCE NOTES

Introduction: A Much More Exciting Game Comes to Pass

1. Quoted in Cliff Christl, "Don Hutson," Green Bay Packers. www.packers.com.
2. Quoted in Bill Huber, "Remembering the Unparalleled Dominance of Don Hutson," *Sports Illustrated,* June 26, 2022. www.si.com.
3. Quoted in Pro Football Hall of Fame, "Greatest Game Ever Played," January 1, 2005. www.profootballhof.com.
4. Quoted in Pro Football Hall of Fame, "Sid Gillman." www.profootballhof.com/players/sid-gillman/.

Chapter One
Men of Steel: Terry Bradshaw and Lynn Swann

5. Quoted in *Golden Football Magazine,* "NFL Championship Games." https://goldenrankings.com/SuperBowl10-C.htm.
6. Quoted in Larry Schwartz, "MVP Swann Super in Steelers Win," ESPN, November 19, 2003. www.espn.com.
7. Quoted in *Sports Illustrated* staff, "Hello, Remember Me? Cowboys Charlie Waters and Cliff Harris Can't Quite Forget Steeler Lynn Swann, Not After What He Did to Them in Super Bowl X," *Sports Illustrated* Vault, January 1979. https://vault.si.com.
8. Quoted in *Time,* "Sport: Super Duel at the Super Bowl," January 1979. https://time.com.
9. Quoted in *Time,* "Sport."

Chapter Two
49ers Strike Gold: Joe Montana and Jerry Rice

10. Quoted in Joe Hession, "75 for 75: The Drive," 49ers Museum, December 8, 2021. www.49ers.com.
11. Quoted in David Bonilla, "Joe Montana or Steve Young? 49ers Great Jerry Rice Makes His Choice," 49ers Webzone, April 2, 2024. www.49erswebzone.com.
12. Quoted in Ryan Gaydos, "Jerry Rice Recalls NFL Draft Worries: 'I Never Thought I Was Going to Get Drafted,'" Fox News, April 20, 2022. www.foxnews.com.
13. Quoted in Jim Owczarski, "Joe Montana, Jerry Rice and What Could Have Been for Bengals in the '80s," *Cincinnati Enquirer,* June 30, 2017. www.cincinnati.com.
14. Quoted in Jason Fitz, "Jerry Rice on What Made Joe Montana So Great and His Favorite Super Bowl Memory," Yahoo Sports Videos, February 7, 2024. https://sports.yahoo.com.

Chapter Three
Return to Glory: Troy Aikman and Michael Irvin

15. Quoted in Jaime Aron, "Aikman, Emmitt, Irvin: Three of a Kind," *The Oklahoman*, September 20, 2005. www.oklahoman.com.
16. Quoted in Joe Drape, "Aikman and Irvin: Two for the Money," *New York Times,* September 11, 1997. www.nytimes.com.
17. Quoted in Tom Friend, "Playmakers: A One-Two Punch Knocks Out the Bills," *New York Times,* February 1, 1993. www.nytimes.com.
18. Quoted in Drape, "Aikman and Irvin."

19. Quoted in Nikki Chavanelle, "Troy Aikman Discusses How to Manage the Personality of Michael Irvin," On 3 Media, May 29, 2023. www.on3.com.

Chapter Four
Colts Connection: Peyton Manning and Marvin Harrison

20. Quoted in NBC Sports, "Peyton Manning: My Record with Marvin Harrison Won't Be Broken," *Pro Football Talk* (blog), March 18, 2016. www.nbcsports.com.
21. Quoted in Kevin Bowen, "Peyton Manning on Marvin Harrison: 'He Truly Was One of a Kind,'" Colts.com, August 6, 2016. www.colts.com.
22. Quoted in CBS News, "Colts Trample Chargers," September 26, 1999. www.cbs news.com.
23. Quoted in WAVE3.com, "Peyton, Harrison Chasing New Title: NFL's Best Combo Ever," September 17, 2005. www.wave3.com.
24. Quoted in Tampa Bay Buccaneers, "10-06-2003: Post Game Quotes," October 6, 2003. www.buccaneers.com.
25. Quoted in Associated Press, "Duo Breaks Record for TD Passes Between QB, WR," ESPN, October 18, 2005. www.espn.com.

Chapter Five
Patriots Prestige: Tom Brady and Rob Gronkowski

26. Quoted in Khari A. Thompson, "Rob Gronkowski Recalls 'Hilarious' Interaction During His First Time Meeting Tom Brady," Boston.com, August 18, 2023. www.boston.com.
27. Quoted in Matt Hladik, "Rob Gronkowski Reveals the Most Mad He Ever Was at Tom Brady," *The Spun* (blog), October 18, 2024. https://thespun.com.
28. Quoted in Thompson, "Rob Gronkowski Recalls 'Hilarious' Interaction During His First Time Meeting Tom Brady."
29. Quoted in Andrea Wurzburger, "Tom Brady and Rob Gronkowski's Friendship Through the Years," *People,* February 2, 2022. https://people.com.
30. Quoted in NBC Sports, "Tom Brady: Rob Gronkowski Is Obviously the Greatest Tight End Ever to Play in the NFL," *Pro Football Talk* (blog), December 9, 2021. www.nbc sports.com.
31. Quoted in Zack Cox, "Rob Gronkowski Explains What Makes Playing with Tom Brady So Much Fun," New England Sports Network, January 24, 2019. https://nesn.com.

Chapter Six
Hail to the Chiefs: Patrick Mahomes and Travis Kelce

32. Quoted in Jillian Nachtigal, "Former Patriots Tight End Rob Gronkowski Reveals a Surprising Opinion Surrounding Travis Kelce," Pro Football & Sports Network, February 5, 2024. www.profootballnetwork.com.
33. Quoted in Kristopher Knox, "Are Patrick Mahomes, Travis Kelce the Top Duo in NFL History After Super Bowl LVIII?," Bleacher Report, February 12, 2024. https://bleacher report.com.
34. Quoted in Adam Teicher, "Why Chiefs' Patrick Mahomes-to-Travis Kelce Connection Is the Best of Its Time," ESPN, February 1, 2021. www.espn.com.
35. Quoted in Teicher, "Why Chiefs' Patrick Mahomes-to-Travis Kelce Connection Is the Best of Its Time."
36. Quoted in Jordan Foote, "Super Bowl LVIII MVP Patrick Mahomes After KC Chiefs' Win: 'We're Not Done,'" *Sports Illustrated,* February 12, 2024. www.si.com.
37. Quoted in Jori Epstein, "Inside Patrick Mahomes' and Travis Kelce's Perfect Night to Carry the Chiefs to Another Super Bowl," Yahoo! Sports, January 29, 2024. https://sports.yahoo.com.

FOR FURTHER RESEARCH

Books

Josh Anderson, *G.O.A.T. Football Tight Ends*. Minneapolis: Lerner, 2024.

Josh Anderson, *G.O.A.T. Football Wide Receivers.* Minneapolis: Lerner, 2024.

Tyler Dunne, *The Blood and Guts: How Tight Ends Save Football*. New York: Twelve, 2022.

Lew Freedman, *Caught by Don Hutson! A Biography of Pro Football's First Modern Receiver.* Jefferson, NC: McFarland, 2022.

Percy Leed, *Peyton Manning: Most Valuable Quarterback.* Minneapolis: Lerner, 2022.

Joseph Levit, *Meet Tom Brady: Tampa Bay Buccaneers Superstar.* Minneapolis: Lerner, 2022.

Alexander Lowe, *G.O.A.T. Football Quarterbacks*. Minneapolis: Lerner, 2023.

Ryan G. Van Cleave, *Travis Kelce: Superstar Tight End*. Mankato, MN: Capstone, 2024.

Internet Sources

Kevin Bowen, "Peyton Manning on Marvin Harrison: 'He Truly Was One of a Kind,'" Colts.com, August 6, 2016. www.colts.com.

Joe Drape, "Aikman and Irvin: Two for the Money," *New York Times*, September 11, 1997. www.nytimes.com.

Tom Friend, "Playmakers: A One-Two Punch Knocks Out the Bills," *New York Times*, February 1, 1993. www.nytimes.com.

Joe Hession, "75 for 75: The Drive," 49ers Museum, December 8, 2021. www.49ers.com.

Bill Huber, "Remembering the Unparalleled Dominance of Don Hutson," *Sports Illustrated*, June 26, 2022. www.si.com.

Kristopher Knox, "Are Patrick Mahomes, Travis Kelce the Top Duo in NFL History After Super Bowl LVIII?," Bleacher Report, February 12, 2024. https://bleacherreport.com.

Christopher Price, "Rob Gronkowski Explains Why He Came Out of Retirement and How He Ended Up with the Buccaneers," Boston.com, April 22, 2020. www.boston.com.

Sports Illustrated staff, "Hello, Remember Me? Cowboys Charlie Waters and Cliff Harris Can't Quite Forget Steeler Lynn Swann, Not After What He Did to Them in Super Bowl X," *Sports Illustrated* Vault, January 1979. https://vault.si.com.

Time, "Sport: Super Duel at the Super Bowl," January 1979. https://time.com.

Khari A. Thompson, "Rob Gronkowski Recalls 'Hilarious' Interaction During His First Time Meeting Tom Brady," Boston.com, August 18, 2023. www.boston.com.

Websites

NFL.com

www.nfl.com
This online home for the National Football League includes individual player statistics, game schedules, links to purchase tickets, and a fan store.

Pro Football Hall of Fame

www.profootballhof.com
The Pro Football Hall of Fame showcases the rich history of the sport from its beginnings. The website provides a survey of great moments in football history, a searchable database of the nearly four hundred players inducted into the hall, and more.

Pro Football Reference

www.pro-football-reference.com
This in-depth and well-organized website specializes in statistics. Here, football fans can search by team or yearly leaders in nearly every defensive and offensive category. Who led the NFL in rushing or sacks this season? Which quarterback completed the most passes in 1966? Who holds the record for kicking the longest field goal in NFL history? It is all here.

INDEX

PICTURE CREDITS

Cover: Steve Jacobson/Shutterstock

6: Ringo Chiu/Shutterstock
9: Associated Press
15: Associated Press
19: Associated Press
21: Associated Press
23: Associated Press
27: Associated Press
30: Associated Press
35: Associated Press
37: Associated Press
43: Associated Press
45: Associated Press
51: Associated Press
53: Jason Pohuski/Cal Sport Media/Newscom
56: Associated Press

ABOUT THE AUTHOR

Dominick Reston lives in Southern California and writes for both adults and young adults.